orth America

RICAN BISON

by Tyler Omoth

FOCUS
READERS

North Star
EDITIONS

www.northstareditions.com

Produced for North Star Editions by Red Line Editorial.

Photographs ©: D. M. Baker/iStockphoto, cover, 1; Volodymyr Burdiak/ Shutterstock Images, 4–5, 27 (middle left); Betty4240/iStockphoto, 7; Eduard Kyslynskyy/Shutterstock Images, 10–11; Moisieiev Igor/Shutterstock Images, 12–13; Nagel Photography/Shutterstock Images, 15; Eric Isselee/Shutterstock Images, 17; Bonnie Fink/Shutterstock Images, 18–19; Scott Walton/iStockphoto, 21; thejack/iStockphoto, 22; Darren Baker/Shutterstock Images, 24–25; lemonflash/iStockphoto, 27 (top); Rusty Dodson/Shutterstock Images, 27 (middle right); Jedi Len/iStockphoto, 27 (bottom), 29

ISBN
978-1-63517-029-0 (hardcover)
978-1-63517-085-6 (paperback)
978-1-63517-188-4 (ebook pdf)
978-1-63517-138-9 (hosted ebook)

Library of Congress Control Number: 2016951023

Printed in the United States of America
Mankato, MN
November, 2016

About the Author

Tyler Omoth is the author of more than two dozen books for children. He loves going to sporting events and taking in the sun at the beach. Omoth lives in sunny Brandon, Florida, with his wife, Mary.

TABLE OF CONTENTS

CHAPTER 1

WHERE THE BISON ROAM

Long ago, millions of American bison roamed the plains. They used to roam freely across most of the United States and Canada.

Today, approximately 500,000 American bison live in North America.

But in the 1800s, humans killed as many as 50 million bison for food and sport.

Today most bison live in national parks. They also live on farms. In these places, they are protected from hunters. Large, thundering **herds** of bison live

FUN FACT

Bison are commonly called buffalo, but this name is incorrect. Buffalo are an African animal.

A herd of bison grazes in Yellowstone National Park.

in Yellowstone National Park in Wyoming. Others live in Wood Buffalo National Park in Canada.

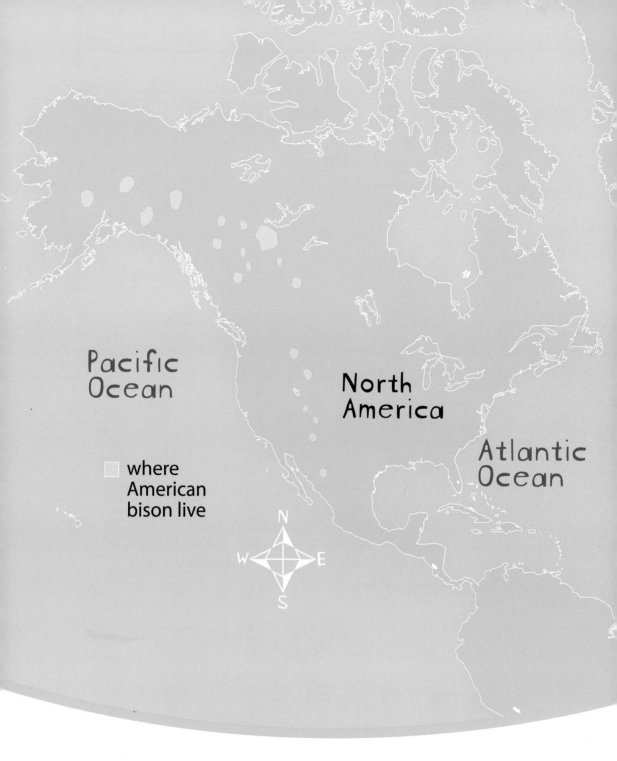

Pacific
Ocean

North
America

Atlantic
Ocean

☐ where
American
bison live

N
W E
S

American Bison now live in national parks and on farms.

American bison live in areas where there is plenty of grass and other plants to eat. They are **herbivores**. Plains and lightly wooded areas are ideal places for the herds to gather.

FUN FACT

In the wild, bison live to be approximately 12 to 20 years old.

SHAPING THE PLAINS

Before they were hunted to near extinction, American bison helped shape the Great Plains. They did this by changing the **ecology**. Their hooves moved the soil, helping plants grow. As herbivores, bison graze on grasses. With the short grass, prairie dogs could look out for **predators**. Wolves also relied on bison. Bison were one of their most common food sources.

American bison helped shape the Great Plains landscape by eating and trimming down the grasses.

CHAPTER 2

NORTH AMERICA'S LARGEST MAMMAL

The American bison is the largest **mammal** in North America. A bison's head is very large. It is covered in thick brown fur. A furry beard hangs down.

Measuring to the top of the shoulder, some bison can grow to be 6.5 feet (2.0 m) tall.

Both males and females have two small, curved horns. Bison use their heads and sharp horns for ramming. They ram against predators to protect themselves. Male bison also ram into each other in competition. Behind the bison's head is a large

FUN FACT

Male bison compete for the attention of females. They butt their large heads against each other and **bellow** loudly.

> Two male bison fight for females during mating season.

shoulder hump. The bison's hump is made mostly of strong muscle.

Broad shoulders make bison look large and powerful. Their bodies are slim from the shoulders to the tails. The back of a bison's body is built for speed. The slender body also helps bison jump, spin, and swim.

The bison may be big, but it can move quickly. While a bison can

FUN FACT

Bison roll in the dirt, making bare spots on the prairie. This helps them get rid of bugs and shed loose fur.

PARTS OF AN AMERICAN BISON

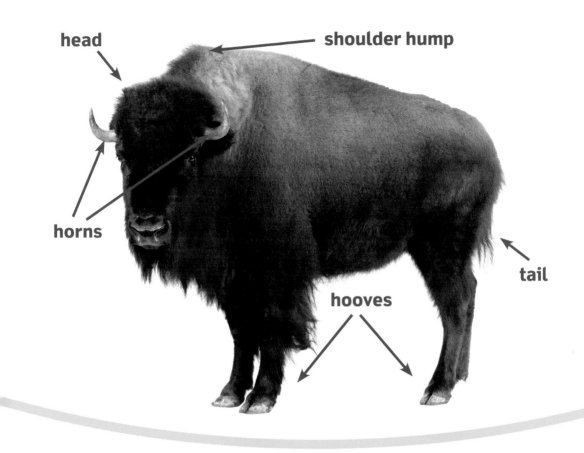

head

shoulder hump

horns

tail

hooves

weigh more than 2,000 pounds (907 kg), it can run as fast as 40 miles per hour (65 km/h). That is as fast as most horses.

CHAPTER 3

SURVIVING IN THE WILD

American bison feed mostly on grasses, shrubs, and twigs. They eat during the morning and evening. In the winter, heavy snow makes it difficult for bison to find food.

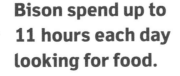

Bison spend up to 11 hours each day looking for food.

Bison **regurgitate** partly digested food, called cud, from their stomachs. They chew it while resting. Doing this helps them digest their food more easily.

Bison are well equipped to survive in North America's changing

FUN FACT

A bison's fur is so thick and insulating that snow on a bison's back will not melt. The fur keeps the bison's body heat in and the cold out.

Bison need thick fur to keep them warm in the bitterly cold winters.

seasons. A bison's fur is very thick.

The fur is especially thick around

the bison's head and shoulders.

 A herd of bison face off against a hungry wolf.

Bison often huddle together during winter storms to keep each other warm.

Because they are so big, bison have few natural predators. But hungry wolves, bears, and mountain lions sometimes attack.

When threatened, bison form a large circle. They put the **calves** in the middle. The adult bison stand around them with their large heads facing the predator.

CHAPTER 4

BISON LIFE

Bison calves are born in the spring. Each female bison usually has only one calf. The newborn does not have the noticeably large head or shoulder hump. Those develop over time.

A calf stays near its mother for protection.

Mothers raise their calves until they are approximately 8 to 12 months old. A calf feeds on its mother's milk until it is ready to eat grass. The father does not help the mother raise the **offspring**.

Bison spend most of the year living in small groups. They come together during the mating season.

FUN FACT

Newborn bison are sometimes called "red dogs" because of their reddish-brown color.

AMERICAN BISON LIFE CYCLE

Calves are born in spring and can stand shortly after birth.

Calves drink their mother's milk until they are ready to eat grass.

Adult bison can live and survive on their own.

By the middle of their first winter, calves start to eat on their own.

FOCUS ON
AMERICAN BISON

Write your answers on a separate piece of paper.

1. Summarize Chapter 3 of this book.

2. Do you think humans should have hunted so many bison? Why or why not?

3. Bison eat grass and other plants. They are:
   A. herbivores
   B. omnivores
   C. carnivores

4. When threatened by predators, why do you think bison form a circle and face outward?
   A. By forming a circle, they are helping keep warm.
   B. By facing the predator, they can easily charge at it with their horns.
   C. By facing outward, they can more easily run away.

5. What does **relied** mean in this book?

    A. ran away from

    B. did not need

    C. depended on

Wolves also **relied** on bison. Bison were one of their most common food sources.

6. What does **roamed** mean in this book?

    A. traveled to a specific location for a reason

    B. traveled without a plan or purpose

    C. traveled with a specific plan or purpose

Long ago, millions of American bison **roamed** the plains. They used to roam freely across most of the United States and Canada.

Answer key on page 32.

GLOSSARY

bellow
A deep roaring sound made by a person or animal.

calves
Babies or young bison.

ecology
The relationship of living things to one another and their surroundings.

herbivores
Animals that only eat plants and not meat.

herds
Groups of animals that stay together.

mammal
An animal that gives birth to live babies, has fur or hair, and produces milk.

offspring
The babies of any animal.

predators
Animals that hunt other animals for food.

regurgitate
To bring food that has been swallowed back up to the mouth.

TO LEARN MORE

BOOKS

Anthony, David. *Bison.* New York: PowerKids Press, 2016.

Graubart, Norman D. *Bison in American History.* New York: PowerKids Press, 2015.

Hirsch, Rebecca E. *Bison: A Winter Journey.* New York: AV2 by Weigl, 2017.

NOTE TO EDUCATORS

Visit **www.focusreaders.com** to find lesson plans, activities, links, and other resources related to this title.

INDEX

Answer Key: 1. Answers will vary; **2.** Answers will vary; **3.** A; **4.** B; **5.** C; **6.** B